I LOST SOMEONE THEN FOUND THEM IN MY BODY

By the same author:

Poetry:

Exit Wounds
Letters to my Lover from a Small Mountain Town
Thirsting for Lemonade
Meanwhile, the Oak
Rhymes with Hyenas
Alternative Hollywood Ending

Novels:

Pursuing Love and Death
Jean Harley was Here
Little Bit

I LOST SOMEONE THEN FOUND THEM IN MY BODY

HEATHER TAYLOR-JOHNSON

RECENT
WORK
PRESS

I Lost Someone Then Found Them in My Body
Recent Work Press
Canberra, Australia

Copyright © Heather Taylor-Johnson, 2026

ISBN: 9781764106856 (paperback)

A catalogue record for this book is available from the National Library of Australia

All rights reserved. This book is copyright. Except for private study, research, criticism or reviews as permitted under the Copyright Act, no part of this book may be reproduced, stored in a retrieval system, or transmitted in any form by any means without prior written permission. Enquiries should be addressed to the publisher.

Cover image: © D-Mo, 2025. Reproduced with permission.
Set by Recent Work Press

recentworkpress.com

*In memory of my dear friend Alison Flett
and Tom the dog—good boy*

Contents

I FOUND THEM

A Conversation about Art	3
Games	6
Holding Water	8
We have to try harder to stop trying so hard	10
After Suzanne Duchamp's *Young Woman with Dog*	12
Distraction	14
Spoonbridge and Cherry at the Opening of a Toilet	15
But how did the hole get there?	16
Permanence	17
House on Stilts	18
Briefly	20
Tarragon	22
Mine, in three parts	23

SOMEONE I LOST

If You Come Back	29
Clouds	30
Bobo	32
I've Forgotten to Talk about Fire	34
Hello / Goodbye	35
Nothing Out Of The Ordinary	37
When You Go We Are Left	39
Windsong	40
Safe	41

IN MY BODY

Dancing to Flo Rida with Julia Gillard (Ladie's Night at the Vic no. 2)	45
No Matter How Much Skin I Lose I Am Always the Same Body	49
the room closes in	50
But It's Not Just When Your Period Stops	52
'The Song Remains the Same'	56
Freezeframe the Bear	57
'Pain cannot be told. Yet, in isolation, it grows.'	58
Softly	59
When Things Fall Apart	62
How to Heal Yourself	63
Crisis / Disease	66
Diagnosis and Treatment	67
Bath Towel	68
Some Questions I Ask Myself When I Cannot Sleep	69

I FOUND THEM

A Conversation about Art

What are your thoughts on art and the female body?

> My parents used to have a large painting above their bed in which a naked man and woman sat upright, as if they were dancers about to rise in a single gesture, though their legs were bent over and under the other's. Their fingers sensed and sculpted the other's face, their hair long and free in a reflection of the times—it was only an outline, this painting of lovers, a few curving strokes in the pervasive brown-on-cream of the 70s, and I was too young to know what could happen if the image had been fleshed out, yet there was something naughty about the act of looking at it, even though I knew the couple were probably married which made it okay because that's how my world treated me, the two-story home where everyone had their own rooms but my parents chose to share one, their low murmur at night, the time I walked in on their nakedness and my mother's quick roll to her side of the bed, her quicker laugh. Each time I entered their room, aside from the time I just mentioned, the first thing I saw was the painting and my heart beat fast, and when my eyes found the woman's breast, it calmed.

So you were, what, six? seven?

> I must've been eight, too young to have adopted a female gaze and contemplated how it made me feel. I thought of the subjects as my mother and father, and I loved my mother's breasts. The fat ease of them. The generous heft. The rise and the rest of the familiar and unknown. As a child, when she changed her clothes in front of me or came out of the shower, her naked breasts held my future. I thought *this is a woman's body I will one day understand*, and now that she's seventy-two, it's the same.

Do you wish you could see the woman's breast in this photograph?

> It would take the focus away from her torso and I think the photo's about guts or maybe fallopian tubes, which is much more centre-of-the-world, thematically, so no, I don't need to see her breast. It's like asking if I'd like to see the other side of the moon when I'm perfectly enchanted by the side that's glowing in front of me. Of course I know the shadowed-moon is just as beautiful as the surface we can see, but it's not what the moment's about.

Why do you think the woman is lying on the ground, naked and curled around a bowl of eels?

> Either she's ill because she's already eaten from the bowl or she's exhausted from having birthed eels, and maybe it doesn't matter because the two can be the same in the way that the dark and the bright sides of the moon are more or less the same. Regardless, the fact that the eels are in a bowl keeps everything clean. Not that I think art should be clean, but I do think naked is the cleanest form of woman.

Do you mean 'the purest'?

> I mean a superlative, yes. I once read a book where a mother, in a fit of madness, makes herself ill by overeating eels. I'm not sure if it was an act of confusion or extreme clarity but it'd certainly be interesting to ask the author what he'd meant by introducing eels. He was a man, though; he might've meant something altogether separate from what his female character intended. I myself have never eaten an eel or even seen an eel but I can grasp the metaphorical possibilities: the eels in the bowl, eels in the body, the eel behind the man's leg of the painting in my parents' room.

If you were the subject in the photograph, what would we see in the bowl?

> Bloody placenta, though let me digress: everything little I could gather of my children—their nail clippings, hair trimmings, their baby teeth and the plastic pegs that held their bellybuttons into shape after their bodies were cut from the bloody placenta that my body grew to grow them. The black stumps of their bellybuttons that fell off the pegs.

When you look at a photo of a naked woman in an artwork, do you ever think of ghosts?

> In this case, sepia has a lot to answer for but so does the patriarchy. The photograph we're talking about was taken by a female, but there is always a man outside the image presenting us with eels. In the example of the painting above my parents' bed, the feeling I had while taking it in might have been ethereal, yes. Thoughts I couldn't form and emotions I couldn't name thickened the room as a ghost might, but the breast always brought me back to my mother, the solidity of her. Perhaps the question should be 'When you look at a photo of a naked woman in an artwork, do you think of your mother?'

That's a valid question.

> So do you?

The photograph is 'Untitled', from the Eel Series by Francesca Woodman, 1978
The book is *Tin Drum* by Gunter Grass, 1959

Games

Days pinch and lately I've noticed every time I look in the mirror
I'm squinting—maybe it's a grimace. Without trying
I've mastered the façade of a Besser block threatened by a mallet,
by which I mean maybe the world won't kill me but it'll definitely hurt
and I've got to be ready. I'm afraid of routine. Give me something easy
like a boardgame and I'll show you anxiety. When I was a kid I played
boardgames all the time because I'm competitive but not sporty.
I like showing off, but only if it's part of the rules.
I consider aiming to win the number one rule in a boardgame.
Not in raising a child, though. Or in writing a poem. I liked the game
Sorry because of its name. It's almost the opposite of *Thank You*
so it felt sort of rebellious. I also liked it because of the smooth
bright plastic pawns that fitted just-so in my small fingers.
My dad once threw his across the room during family game night
and maybe that's why: his fingers were too grown-up thick and clumsy.
Chance was fun when I was eight but I feel like the mere thought of it
could kill me now. Honestly, what out there is safe? The other day
I saw a woman trip and fall hard on the footpath because the root of a tree
had pushed skyward to meet her. This is what it's come to. Like the game
Snakes and Ladders, we're only ever wanting to move forward
but maybe we should tip-toe so the slides won't hear us and the roots
won't feel us coming. I think I need a better plan. It's so hard making art
with these worldly distractions. I wish I could mould each and every one of them
to work *with* me and *for* me. I wish I could hustle my environment—
the insatiable clouds, the humping waves, the treacherous weeds
at our back door. Oh, and every abandoned warehouse, which my youngest
son would definitely buy because he loves *Monopoly*. He is always the banker
and owns the most property and has all the wealth, no matter who his opponent is.
I think he cheats constantly. It's the same with cards. I want to give him
the benefit of the doubt because he has excellent spatial reasoning
so he literally sees possibility, but let's be honest, he's a spiv, which is fortunate
for him and sometimes makes me proud. It seems as though he doesn't feel

the pinch but in saying that, I am definitely a bad mother. My mood
could be my hormone levels fluctuating like a windsock, filling
and falling as it picks up 40-knot gusts. Weather has a lot to do with it.
I think my brother cheated at *Monopoly* too. He's a banker now, I do not lie.
I never liked playing with him because of course he always won but also
I didn't much care about money. I want more money, obviously, but it's not
something I see or touch very often, and how would I get it if cheating
isn't in my blood? Unless we're counting my brother and my son,
in which case it is. But even in a card game I've never cheated.
I respect the actual cards too much, like photographs and books.
I love holding visuals close to my chest and I love keeping secrets.
My favourite card game is gin. My favourite drink is wine.
I think I would presently play more cards if I could only drink less wine.
It started at such a young age, though most would say 16 is ripe.
Hello, beer pong? Is that you? It was hard to tell because I usually
passed out directly after meeting it. Like cheating, I cannot skull,
but isn't that what we're either seeking or dreading these days:
obliteration? When I think about what obliteration might look like
it makes me want to come up with a new game that involves only the stars
and our thoughts. In the instructions it would say to hold the stars
close to your chest and keep your thoughts a secret. I'd call it *You're Welcome*.

Holding Water

In my dreams I'm often running away
or driving a car down a hill, out of control.
I think I'd be calmer if I dreamt I was on water.

Because I can't afford the sea
I count sweet blessings in the bath.
Drawn to it when I'm ill, I have a tin full of oils,
a lover who helps me rise when I've had enough.

When I was a child, I swam circles around a canoe
where my father and brother had dropped their lines.
We're here to catch dinner so give us a wide berth—
I thought he meant *birth*, imaged a school of fish
shimmering wildly between my legs.

I wish I could remember the first time I swam in water,
which was a lake, I know. Unless we are talking
about a womb, which is close to a lake.
Tonight I want to dream I am close to a lake.

Lakes have borders and water does not.
How to hold water?
By opening the top of your praying hands.
By shaping a cup of your hankering mouth.
In a tissue. In a tank. In a body. In a bath.

Most people don't know who owns the water,
only that it's regulated so there must be an owner.
The cod owns the Murray, and the crayfish
and the perch and the gudgeons and the yabbies
and short-necked turtles and rainbow trout.

In Clayton Bay, where the river becomes
lake / becomes sea / becomes whole of the world,
we are known as the family who swim together,
the meaty reeded snakes surfing our waves.

We have to try harder to stop trying so hard

Sometimes I say your name and wonder if I'm talking to myself.
How long has it been this way, me tugging at the small tangle
between my chest and throat, complicating speech? I don't know
what I'll do if I ever loosen it enough to let go. What does anyone
do with anything these days? Hound it? Isolate it? *Post it. Eat it.*

Words are becoming indefinable, leaving us only with our faces
and this botched-up view. In their hurry to escape, words
have smudged the windows. Outside someone is walking a dog
and when our words fly away with the insects heading towards
the water, I'd like one to land in the thick of its coat, that way
when the dog barks, it might translate what we don't say.

We haven't showered for days, rather dive into water, rather
stride dripping home. Our words are drowned. They are melting
in this heatwave. They're in bird droppings and resting in the soft
nests of twigs, feathers and tiny strips of worn plastic.
Cockatoo song everywhere come evening.

Our rainbow peace flag is flapping in the wind.
We got it from Woodstock, then had lunch then
found a swimming hole with the kind of waterfall
you can sit under and in and we did. It's often about water,
and words, which are now caught in the fabric of the flag.

When we notice our words disappearing, should we run after them
waving? Or close our eyes so it's not a lasting memory.
We could welcome their future ghosts by holding hands
in acquiescence, or reconsider history, read more widely,
meditate—I don't see how any of it would help.

If it were me disappearing I'd want a farewell party.

If it were you disappearing, can't imagine the reds of my eyes.

I realise how wrong this is—I'm looking at the vast water,
not magnifying our surrounds. What about in the bathroom,
where our toothbrushes lie? What about in the fingerprints
on the remote control? Our words in the house of our living,
in the direct path my eyes take to get to yours, in the eggs
I bought and the bickies and corn nuts we eat. Our words
in the stomachs of our hunger. In the clothes you hung
and I took down and we put away to wear later. They'll rest
in the folds of our elbows and knees. In the grit and dust that stick
to our heels then detach every night when we crawl into bed.
Our words wrapped tightly in the blankets of our skin.

After Suzanne Duchamp's *Young Woman with Dog*

1.
The first dog is
self-pillow repose,
as if under moon shadow
dreaming of moon.

The moon is
paper glow so low –
I thought I heard it calling
to the dog's sleeping ghost.

The ghost is
the inverse image
filling in the sweeping gaps
and all its lonely folk.

2.
The second dog is
impossible chair:
upright base of benevolence,
could break under trust.

Trust is
eye to eye instants
—*whose turn is it, mine or yours?*
those words don't matter.

What matters is
war and cancer and
the tiny dead mouse,
plants, sex and hands.

3.
The third dog is
chasing the bird lift,
sniffing wood in rain shower,
length stretched to fit bed.

The bed is
holding the toxins
of the earth's longest weekday –
the deep sink harvesting gut.

The gut is
good gaseous churn,
the universe trapped inside
the deep snoring core.

4.
The fourth dog is
curling eye-level,
a masterpiece on the wall
absorbing our sigh.

Our sigh is
all we cannot keep,
the questionable and done,
the gift and the harm.

Harm is
human unkindness;
once too-far gets far-too-close;
opposite of dog.

Distraction

1.
After the heatwave, I sit in the shade on a lounge mat,
the flies testing its plasticity: journal, water, half a punnet
of sliced strawberries, the neighbourhood rooster
gleeful and randy, the wind flicking leaves over my head.
Shy and small, I remember your hands on me
and that I have a deadline that isn't about you.

2.
I can clean a kitchen, eyes closed, but it doesn't mean I dream of it.
The ant has found the brown smear, the cloth has ruined
their collage, dinner plates chase the breakfast bowls.
Time sits, entirely gendered, like an old man in a cushioned chair,
resigned to watching patterns. I wipe down what's become loose,
scrub at what's determined to stay. I meant to write a poem today.

Spoonbridge and Cherry at the Opening of a Toilet

'I will go to the opening of anything, including a toilet seat'—Andy Warhol

It was JB's birthday, everyone was there but her ex, who I most wanted to see,
half-empty crystal glasses littering the table, confident guests circling,
holding the half-full, the slosh of constant conversation, gesticulations,
moles, gold, you said to me *I just love tonight, it's the best night of my life*
and I adored the overstatement because I'm always on your side, I said
Mine too though it came off as eager because I'm usually unsophisticated,
wish I was ten years older or ten years younger than I am right now.

HK entered the room, the only one wearing a three-piece suit, and Lady B
was smoking cigarillos from a fancy silver flip-top case, twitching her nose
and scratching her leg—*Do the streets feel like conveyor belts?*
Do you miss your mother? What was the name of that album with the guy
holding the cabbage head?—you reached into the volcano
of meatballs, flicked your wrist at the gherkins, cocked a brow
as Triple Threat scooped nuts from a bowl shaped like a penis and told us
she'd been to the sea, *Just look at my tan!* but she's partial to make-up
that lightens her complexion, so yeah, when she walked away
in her red jumpsuit I thought of that giant cherry and spoon sculpture
in the city where my mother grew up; I do miss her, since you asked.

You were scanning, scanning, you're always scanning, you once told me
you viewed the world as miniature snapshots sewn together with fine thread
then projected as a silent film, *Last night I crawled into bed at seven*
o'clock and slept until nine this morning, I told you I was streaming
a documentary series and you said *Oh I know, it can be so hard*, the music
grew too loud for me to hear what you said next but when you nodded
toward the shirtless man throwing olives in the air then catching them
one by one in his mouth, I understood completely, half-thoughts
and absinthe shots, you said *I'll start craving milk around noon tomorrow*
and I surprised you by touching your arm, *That's a marvellous idea for a poem.*

But how did the hole get there?

'That hole in the wall the size of a head just near the sink
where you found the lollies—I did that. I'd just read
the George Pell verdict and only two nights earlier
watched the doco on Michael Jackson, of course still reeling
from the Weinstein days, pressure building in the air
like muted curse words, tinnitus complaints at every
social gathering. It seemed we all suffered from anxiety
as we schmoozed and drank and we schmoozed and drank
way too much but we didn't know what else to do.
The world felt small, like a single room, too many dust particles
flying around the chandelier, my thin soul, those fat slabs
of cheese tossed into the bin. No one told me how dirty
life can be. No one can possibly count all the wounded
who shadow-watch. My fist shot out and I didn't ask
what any of it meant—there was no time, and I know
that's a lie because time is endless. Imagine asking
the survivors of George Pell what they have to say about time—
still, there was no *time*, and when my children asked me
about the hole I told them I honestly didn't know how it got there
and I honestly do not. I told them maybe the house is just old,
even walls eventually crumble and break, which they accepted
because they're kids, and now they use it for hiding their lollies.'

Permanence

> —*When asked what type of books he might write when he retires, academic and revered novelist Brian Castro responded (to the effect), 'Whatever I want! The books they wouldn't have wanted me to write while I was here!'*

Yes, they had stapled your clothes to the floor with Officeworks supplies.
Sometimes it was so difficult to move you couldn't stop the words
from flying round the room and landing on your nose then fluttering
off to bury their mouths, the carpet a mausoleum of your untold stories,
disembodied feathers everywhere. Now that you're home, who needs clothes?
You left them behind in the outline of your body, the spectres fallen
to their knees to round up the old gold staples. Rumour has it they're reusing
each one to build redgum bookshelves in all of Australia's universities.
You snigger, completely naked. You're writing on your skin in permanent ink,
movement and danger so impressed they do anything you ask.

House on Stilts

It isn't the beginning but start with this morning. Finally sun,
and the windows of this home away from home, the bed holding me,
a book, inevitably, and my dog Tom, old and sleeping-in.

At lunch, repetition is easy as I sit and read and write and eat.
The lake is a cool reflection of clouds heaving stillness.
Nothing can ever truly go away, can it?

My dog and I amble. At thirteen he trots with his tongue
hanging low, his muzzle and underbelly completely white
while I'm forty-seven and breathe full-chested on the rise.

If I move backwards to yesterday, we are still not at the beginning.
But where would that be? When I looked down at your face
and said we were a team? Birth is spectacular and something we own.

On the path that hugs the cliffs of the lake I unclip his lead, pure dog
in the open wild. Most people call it a river. Let's settle for a large body
of freshwater somewhere in between and know that it's personal.

A holiday home is a home that has less dramatic conditions
than the ones we routinely inhabit. I don't know how to claim space
nor how to let you go, but it seems they both involve this.

Life comes with pivotal moments that separate the lengthening days
and yesterday was one of them, today another, though brighter.
I don't have to be frightened of our fading if it means we get to rebuild.

Here, pelicans keep fishing for their lunch, family cars ferry
kayaks and jet skis to the ramp, my dog sniffs at then pisses on
every clump of green he can, so days stay the same.

Our story is like an old tide calling for new strokes.
We're no more than a house on stilts with a view,
plenty of scope for DIYs, all those years of pottering.

Briefly

A quiet
morning,
the clearing
sky, a Saturday
phone-scroll under
my sick shroud and a
woman in a support group
voicing her dread: she's 8 months
pregnant, how's she going to cope? I want
to tell her that years ago on the 4th Plinth in
Trafalgar Square sat a 13-tonne sculpture called
Alison Lapper Pregnant, the face looking at what
is distant and full, and full white breasts resting on a
jam-packed belly, her marble arms stumped at the
shoulders, her legs unduly small. Disabled or
not, when you're 8 months pregnant
you lead with your belly. I find it
interesting how trust
sprouts there, like fear and sickness sometimes do
which can also be named home. I aim for optimism
most of the time but I can't help being theatrical, I mean

I was the type of expectant mother who entered a room belly first thinking no one else was doing it, anywhere. At night I'd introduce myself to nearly-baby, which gave me nightmares, like fear and sickness sometimes do. I would've asked the support group *how will I cope?* because what kind of mother knocks her baby into a wall while navigating walking down the hall, but social media was still embryonic. Vertigo doesn't hang a sign on its back saying *baby on board* and of course there are the Klimt paintings, which I also thought of mentioning to the woman needing consolation. In *Hope I* a pregnant woman is naked, her belly clearly leading the way though there are shades of the dead following. In *Hope II* a bare-chested woman draped in a falling golden shawl bows her head towards her massive belly, praying perhaps, an odd skull-form peeking out from behind her nearly-baby. Death is always hanging around birth. I remember counting each bruise in the bath, those traces of my illness walking me down the hall. My body was broken, strong, creating, falling, all the more precious because I knew that soon there wouldn't be time to care for myself, the most selfish of chores the woman who posted would probably / should definitely be performing all day. I want to tell her about the new language birth taught me, a first-person singular when talking about sickness and fear, then a change to the plural when speaking of home, but I don't know where the woman lives, or Alison Lapper, or either of the women in *Hope I* and *II*. I type my commiseration in the old language, and the morning's quiet, and the sky is clearing, and my children are teenagers, heavy in their long sleeps, soon to wake to Saturday phone-scrolls in their beds.

Tarragon

In between a creek and an ocean, nestled in the crook of a hairpin curve on what we called our second honeymoon, we went to the shop to stock our kitchen for the next five days of love, thought hard about which herb to buy, so aware it would shine in more than one meal, amazed in our thirties neither of us knew about tarragon—that week, tarragon in pasta and stir fry, us marvelling at fusion and versatility, me thinking of it as flirty and eccentric, slightly unhinged, phrases I've used to describe you, and yet it became 'our herb' with more to follow: our house, our children, our dog, our plans, us at the centre of our exploding, why my favourite lazy morning tastes of an omelette with diced mushroom, bits of bacon, red onion, capsicum and the sweet surprise of tarragon, its leafy sprinkled liquorice especially good after orgasm, when you tell me, sunrise breath and post-sex sweat, to go ahead, read another chapter before I rise, cooking our breakfast will take some time.

Mine, in three parts

I

April 2020: What Was That Chaos?

Those days were defined by my at-home family who ate a lot
and left the proof lying around—smearing knife, plastic wrap, dried
cereal on the floor. I took breaks from cleaning to write about my aunt
(who was actually my husband's aunt but I loved her as if she were my
own and *more than that* I loved the woman because she was my friend).
She was in a home with dementia then, unable to comprehend the measured
distance kept between chairs and why no one came to visit. Her son (my
husband's cousin so not mine but *I love him too*) lives alone which I think
would've been worse than living in a home because where was his human
contact so essential to survival? Every day we were redefining that word.
(I just typed 'world' by mistake.) I had sex with my husband one night
then cuddled my daughter first thing next morning—we were a gluttony
of germs. If one of us went down we all went down and then we'd get well
together, ideally. But he had a dog (back to the cousin who isn't mine)
who was on her very last grey legs and I hoped she'd make it through
the mess because in those early days how awful to have to deal with death
or anything not linked to COVID-19. I'd curse life as if it owed me
something I hadn't yet thought of. It was my single girlfriends I worried
about most: women *hug*, we *need* touch and what if I'd tried to write
about *that*? It would've been impossibly tender and incredibly slow,
a full-pager and one of my best (ideally) but I think I was too anxious
for the job, had upped my intake of the Rolling Stones, was worried
I'd run out of grog. I went to the bottle-o and felt so guilty for getting
in the check-out person's space that I grabbed a chocolate bar
from the display and said *that's for you*. I should dedicate an entire poem
to that moment; you couldn't have dreamt this shit up in the 2010s.
I think about the day my children will sit down with their children
and talk about COVID and the great lockdowns, though you'd hope

they'll come up with a more descriptive phrase for it: *I lived through
the Earth's Last Stand* because maybe that's what the chaos was, Gaia
rescuing her precedence while humans stayed indoors. My eldest
had devoted his teenage years to slowing down climate change
and rested in this theory, never saw him so relaxed, though now
it's back to whetted distress. My younger son wanted help
with a poetry assignment—*now there was something new and never
seen again*—and my Tik Tok daughter interrupted my husband
with dances in his man cave where he held passionate Zoom meetings
with unionists. But it was our dog Tom who was truly most confused.
Never in his twelve years had he had so many pets.

II

August 2020: How One Haibun Fell into the Other

We were in lake and sky territory, between the blues only shades of green and brown if you didn't count the distant houses, though we had to. Just because we no longer saw the people who lived in them doesn't mean they'd disappeared. Nature is most potent when left to itself and when the virus came, cars hibernated, exhausted from years of hard work; factories stopped chain-smoking, the Earth's lungs resting in a small and healthy peace while people died or hunted for tinned tomatoes or stopped walking or let themselves get swallowed up by the hole inside of their homes. It happened, everything tipped sideways.

> We listened to planes
> not slicing the sky; magpies
> were singing, I swear.

My friend understands the search for 'essence of bird', years ago realising people would pay good money to get as close to it as they could. He's a businessman with two airplanes and seven parachutes that continually teach him about flight, and whenever he considers the sky, which is often, he yields to those planes and parachutes respect. My friend passes his knowledge onto others so that they might learn to fly, even while falling, but when the virus came he had to close his hangars: two large chambers echoing defeat. What happened to the people who wanted to fly when suddenly they were earthbound and hidden?

> Bottles dripped and wept
> into puddles at his feet;
> things got slippery.

III

March 2021: When I last came to your house and someone had COVID but neither of us knew and it was okay

Caught in something like mustard haze, infected air but who could tell,
our dinner good, the basil fresh, it seemed there was little to excite us,
the pandemic as tired as lengthy instruction from a rerouting Siri—
when that kind of mood bears down there's nothing for it but to drink
from the puddle you've poured yourself into and question how you got here,
though I guess we both had something to do with that: confessions and opinions,
a history of a hundred other dinners, the opening of our state borders.

I told you respair is an actual word, the return of hope after a time of desolation,
in fact I see all sorts of party favours ghosting you like a veil,
to which you replied *I don't think I've worn the right dress*
and I wondered what I might wear to a party for the end of something not ending.

Then I felt clumsy in my thrift clothes, which until that moment
I hadn't given a thought to, and this is the problem with me
when I'm with you: Bella, I'm such a dag.

Someone had brought out the roasted almonds but neither of us knew who it was;
we were too busy looking at each other, and this is the best thing about us
when we're together: we recognise ourselves.

It was middle of autumn and when evening fell like a worn paper shade
pulled to the sill of a rain-streaked window in an old tin cottage (remember
that house I lived in when we first met?) we settled in, having taken our time.

We sat at the round table and shared an honest bottle of wine and sure enough
we'd forgotten our worries even mattered—mostly it was the ruckus outside
and how we agreed that though the crickets in your backyard
were mimicking their joy spectacularly, your kitchen had it all.

SOMEONE I LOST

If You Come Back

—for Alison Flett

I've found sun, a patch of couch and pillows that make no sense. Death is unexpected, even when you've spent years preparing for it, so I'll tell you the pillows are green and blue and cantaloupe: I want everything to make sense.

If you come back we can share the sun with pillows on our laps. It'll be glamour mixed with comfort, like drinking chai wearing headscarves and oversized cardigans.

Envious, I once told you only the brave wear headscarves. It was so many years before cancer that when you started losing your hair, no one was the wiser.

I have learned that death happens in an instant, even when it drags its legs behind it, but I do not know how many ways a person can smile until, freckle by freckle, they're gone.

If I try to imagine swallowing the sun, it's you who is doing it, not me. It is / you are *beyond*. You could come back as beyond and still I'd know it was you, but I'd never be able to describe your return to anyone other than us. They'd say it was impossible—your ghost walking *through* the door to the chai-scented, sun-drenched room, Docs scuffing black the floorboards, your eyelashes leading the way—though I know it's probable.

Dreams and memory are spook logic, so I'll wait like a cliff shaped by water and wind and yes, sun, wait here with pillows or there by a tree or while catching a train the way we often did. It seemed the station clock always read a minute to departure and we ran for it, laughing though silent, because making noise would've stolen our breath.

There are so many ways to hear you laugh.

You could come back like that.

Clouds

Love is never what you expected, and here we are, different
from rock, nothing like river, closest to cloud forming thick rain.
These days we're giving it so much muscle we're cutting
ourselves on bed springs while sleeping like the dead.

This isn't about death, though mustn't it be? It's coming up on 9/11,
commemoration of a few brutal steps in an epic walk that might conclude
at the end of the world. I think of us, so filled with sheen, sleeping like heroes
when the phone rang, waking us to news of calculated destruction
in my American home 15,000 kilometres away. We turned on the tele,
hours later fucked ourselves back to sleep. Battle and bliss,
we weren't to know the world would never be the same—media, fear,
the expansion of our slithering limbs—and for months, as trails
smouldered and sparked in the politics of aftermath, we were
splash of cloud, whisp of cloud, no rain in sight. Remember
World Trade Centre as Cloud, that series made from white linen strips
pressed onto blue, handcrafted cotton pulp, the Twin Towers, white
and diaphanous, rising into the air and creating an image
of what it dreamed itself to be? Back then, our first family visit
to NYC, we were floating beside it, still dreaming of each other.

This is not a poem about making love because lately we fight,
just look at our eyes nearly swollen shut with togetherness.
Forgive me, but the world is at war, Gaza disembowelled, as if any
one life could be worthless. How do we handle the ongoingness?

I find it sad the artist Christopher Saucedo, whose brother died
when the Twin Towers collapsed, called his original exhibition
September 11, 2011 (please stop saying 9/11) yet we saw the art
in what's famously named the 9/11 Memorial & Museum
where we talked with our children about hope rising from the ruins.
At first I thought that's what this poem was about: you, me,

our heavy need to straighten up and hold on so we can loosen up
and just hold. But it's not. Not when mothers, fathers and children
from Gaza should be walking on our fertile earth but instead
are flanked by smoking clouds, high, so high, the mass of them
looking down at all that we have done, and all that we have not.

Bobo

Her language left China for an eccentric Australian
and found love by the bronze pigs of Rundle Mall.

A word changes meaning when it changes mouths;
love becomes aí, body san tai.

China did not leave her on Rundle Mall
as her husband did when he died.

Her clothes are a country.
Language is a country.
Grief is a country
and a language and a body,
a buttoned red silk shirt.

She dances with pink and yellow fans.
She ties a photo of her husband to an old pram.

She wears a crown of yellow flowers
as she dances by the bronze pigs on Rundle Mall
and it is plain to see that China did not leave.

Grief is a word that can flourish in the hand
like a green and white Chinese fan.

I see her when I come to town
and she makes me want to write a poem,
which is a language and a body
and a ring of flowers.

It is clear we are both devoted to art
and it is clear we are both devoted to love

and it is clear our bodies are our homes
and that we are countries who move like poems.

I've Forgotten to Talk about Fire

I measure heat by distance. For a year I lived in a Colorado mountain town almost 7,000 feet above sea level, and I was hot even in winter, so close to the sun. I forgot to say I was wearing four layers of clothing and thick woollen socks, but the sun—

Because of a disappearing ozone layer, in Australia I measure distance to the sun with numbers slowly being emptied of air. I imagine those who've had homes and family scorched by fire measure heat through loss.

Flame forms and breaks apart at the very same time. What does it mean to be drawn to fire and why doesn't air melt?   (Air melts)

I had a friend in high school whose sister was struck by lightning and her skin turned black but it didn't melt. I'd like to ask my friend if his sister is drawn to or afraid of fire but it feels cold.

I wish I could forget all the times I fell asleep with a campfire still burning, morning waking me with its smoking breath.
                              (I'm a fool having forgotten most.)

My friend who died in the bushfire was a doctor; he used to hydrate himself intravenously after all-nighters; he knew the importance of water; he died in his father's car while his father died on the melted road, the flames forming and breaking apart all around them at the very same time.

I don't ever want to stop talking about fire.

Hello / Goodbye

1.
First film was *The Incredibles*, enormous characters in Elastigirl, Frozone, Jack-Jack Parr and him, an adult baby in the seat next to me. He might not've blinked the entire time, slept three and a half hours that afternoon. Then, months later, when asked if he liked the movie, he began at the beginning and walked in circles, talking his pidgin in a straight line.

2.
Most days brain-heavy and neuronic, he wobbled from all that sped his way, and I, wondering what he dreamed at night, aimed to be his pillow.

3.
He used to sit on the desk, straight-baked chair redundant in its waiting for his small body, a puzzle piece stuck to his shin. The puzzle piece, the loose shavings fallen to the floor, his attempts and tiny failures—all of this.

4.
Sometimes, when I looked at him amid his siblings' hallway protests, the frypan song, the bench mess and blinding lights, I was already thinking of him.

5.
How'd he get those sunlit eyes that saw glitter in dirt then searched for its scientific name? He listened to the earth in its urgent pleading, its rasping and squawking because it, like him, was a feral thing and it, too, was afraid. Soft warrior with plant-shaped heart, he wished he could call the glitter mica but knew it was aluminium and plastic.

6.
That Gorillaz song he played on the piano, that Beatles song, the Beach Boys one, the one he made up about love, that Elton John and Kiki Dee that's pretty jazzy when you take away the lyrics. Contrary to what you think this means, sometimes his music was political.

7.
Radiant child studying and breaking to post about Uyghur sterilisation, ethical, thirsty, a glass of milk beside a bubbleheaded Chris Hemsworth marketed as Thor, a green plate full of paint, Keith Haring doodles in an A4 pad, the coking of coal, the bleaching of reefs, the Amazon burning, the grazing cattle, my son listening to T Rex's *Mambo Sun* for the first time and some Haring-mass beginning to fall onto his back, bent and stretched like a mountain range being pelted by their alligator rain, the strum in time to the Haring-mass pulling its slippery self onto the centre of his disco.

8.
Art. Art. Art. Art.

9.
I would like to meet him in the Post-Impressionist wing or at the abstract painting. I would like to meet him in front of a photo of Keith Haring. I would like to meet him in Melbourne for brunch. I would like to meet him at a kiosk on top of a mountain, or by a lake where we could talk about clouds reflecting on the lake. I would like to meet him at the untended garden. I would like to re-meet him. I would like to meet him at our dog's memorial. I would like us to meet at a monolith and selfie it. I would like to meet him at the cinema with a box of popcorn, three rows from the back or at the Gov—he can choose the band. Or a karaoke bar—I'll choose the first song, probably that one by Elton John and Kiki Dee. I would like to meet him in another country—Vietnam, Kenya, Cuba—where we'd learn new words of greeting and farewell: hola / adios; hujambo / uende salama; chào / chào.

10.
'Hello!'
'Hello.'
'Goodbye.'
'Goodbye.'

Nothing Out Of The Ordinary

We were not skydivers in the 1990s, I did not wear a cream crocheted bikini top, I was not in love for the first time, we didn't talk quietly amongst ourselves in large crowds about sex and its dramas, we did not drink piss-weak beer, we did not pay $16 a jump and there was never a DC-3 or a perfect sunset through its window, we never fell through snow.

We didn't think we owned the tiny piece of sky above the grass and baseball field separated by the hangar where we laid out our parachutes and packed them into nifty rigs, like there was no runway, no windsock, no caravans, and looking down from 12,000 ft we didn't resemble ants.

We didn't burn the old car and breathe it in for days and my clothes never smelled of bonfire, we didn't wake up to the stink of jet fuel or the sound of dual propellers or the natural push toward blue sky, and I never kissed my boyfriend on the mattress on the floor of his gutted pink bus.

When it rained and there was no way we'd lift that plane we did not pile into a van and head to the cinema for *Pulp Fiction* then quote from it for months: *Which parachute is it, my friend?—It's the one that says Bad Motherfucker.*

We would never have said peregrine falcons were cool and the moon did not move into its nearest position to the Earth, which is not called *perigee*, the two words are not similar, I was not so obsessed with Scully and Mulder that I thought I saw a UFO on my first night jump.

I do not think my skydiving days were my salad days, vegetarianism was not a part of my life back then, I don't know how to read clouds and I don't understand what *split second* means, you can't call me fragile, I don't shake my head, I don't remember any of it, and when I think of all the skydivers who smiled at me in freefall it's not you I miss most.

We didn't eat two-minute noodles in between loads, nobody got sunburnt or laid, there weren't wildfires anywhere in the world, I did not acquire mystery bruises, I did not smoke Camel Lights, we never danced to the Beastie Boys on the table and we always talked about the planet.

We did not wear Teva sandals and I do not have a photo proving the point and it would not look amazing in black and white, blown-up and hung on my living room wall and I never felt sorry for the local farmers who had to listen to Cessna climbs, canopy snaps, us yahooing and their dogs barking at every bit of it all weekend long.

I almost never smashed into the ground, not when I jumped, and once I didn't pull too low and there was no sense of ground rush and in fact I've completely forgotten about it so I almost didn't write this poem, but then I thought none of us deserved it, nothing extraordinary happened, I mean no one even died.

When You Go We Are Left

—for Alison Flett, again

We will be left with ourselves, aging by the hour like sunlight
on water, the flicker of crest and trough, the glint and shade
of every day carrying us closer to the edge, further from the past.
For a while we'll be earnest in noticing one another, more forgiving
and giving, and we'll think we have enough. We'll keep you close
by reading your books and reading the books you especially loved
and we'll think of you when we read new books then recommend
them to each other. We'll become better at certain things,
like appreciating insects in pounding rain or relating to holes
because they require space. We'll speak of you during festive times
and gatherings, the loss less dramatic but more sincere as the years
cluster and roil. We'll see our bodies, in their want and tire, as vessels,
as you would and did. Eventually, one of us will write a poem.

Windsong

What is this body but sacked skin,
the bones of my ancestors,
my blood extreme until it's not?

For years I've worked it strong
and rested it languid, filled it and responded
and took note of replication—breath, blink,
bladder push—yet taken it for granted.

Like dying, which sunk friends
to soft shells covered in follicles
that silent-screamed, their pores tiny
thirsting mouths, inside them a sacrifice
of pump and ooze they'd have loved to
squeeze if only to cut off supply.

Today I'm thinking of Sonia, and bodies,
my own a mess of bad decisions
but holding the scars of good ones,
hers an outline of scattered form
cradling wind through the branches of this tree.

It's spring—

these thoughts rise;
these things happen.

Safe

I remember walking with you and a stroller-bound toddler, in my belly a growing human you'd one day decide to sleep with for the rest of your life. Me, I was crying, you would not walk without zigzag-pulling in front of us and I was sleepless, dreamless, slow-motion impatience ripe to bursting, and then it did. Two men stared at me—I wonder if they were worried. Eight months old and confused, I know *you* were. I'm sorry I yelled, the houses with their eye-shaped windows watching us as we unheroically walked by. I still don't know what the fuss was, though I'm certain it was primal. Three months later the third baby came, all of us learning to live together, moving to a solid beat wild on the surface—you tore a handknitted cardigan off the line when we'd abandoned you for the day. I was so upset I said *no no no* but this time I didn't cry. Progress is important in relationships, as is feeling safe.

I have a friend who's built a treehouse high in the gums and the first time she showed me the view you animal-ran up the rungs and joined us on the platform, the leaves reflecting your fear of heights in their tremble as you breathed. Climbing down, I went first, and halfway along you followed me, jumping onto my shoulders, the twenty-kilo bulk of you, us holding on until you realised you could leap to the ground. I was scraped and bruised, such a day of adventure, but that's what you get from the bush. That summer we camped by the sea with friends, all the children wrapped in floaties splashing in the shallows and you lying in the shade of the adult bodies seated in the fold-up chairs. Later there was the jetty, where you had no choice but to jump in after us because you hated being alone more than you hated heights. How you clung to my shoulders, this time not suspended in air but flailing in the water. *Hold on, hold on* I said, and you did until we both calmed and swam together to the shore, where the compact sand was safe.

It was hard being a heavy-duty guard dog in a backyard burdened by tall metal fences, nothing to see but the daily birds, who were okay in the oak tree but warned off from the apricot. Mostly you loved the house by the water, where the upstairs deck wound around the house so you could bark at anyone walking toward you and follow them until they were gone. It was clear to me this was your job, your fear of heights conditional. Sometimes we told you *that's enough* while clapping our hands, but mostly wanted pleasure for you so let you have your way. You were old when we bought that place, sometimes walking so slowly in front of me I thought I might trip over you and at times became impatient, even as you turned to look at me as if to say *you still there?* There were geckos in the bark chips, possums in the tree where each night that we sat by the fire you, sentinel and stealth, stared them down, protecting us from their small and curious foolery. You looked so fine in the hole we dug for you under that tree, and now when night comes, we're safe.

IN MY BODY

Dancing to Flo Rida with Julia Gillard (Ladie's Night at the Vic no. 2)

2010 a debaucherous year abroad, certainly on Thursdays
after Zumba when my sisters and I gathered for Ladies'
Night at the Victoria Hotel—have I told this one before?
Always beer, someone with shots, sparkling eyes,
half-closed lids. I worried about calories even though
we'd just sweated to body-positive songs by Shakira
at the community hall then moved the tables
and continued dancing to east-coast hip-hop at the bar.
I begged for ciggies. I swear I thought I was twenty-two
until the next morning told me otherwise.

Most Fridays I took the baby and her brother for bagels
and green juice once we'd waved goodbye to the eldest
at his school in the mountains: crisp air, climbing wall,
little kids in denim jeans—life was moving, we were all
getting older and I was way past my twenties,
hangovers worse than they'd ever been.

When summer came we were counting tent pegs
and muesli bars for the trip that would gift us new
mountains, and we'd become different people
but continued to paint ourselves with the same old love.
I put the baby down for her morning nap and settled her
brothers in front of a show about animals in a submarine.
Facebook newfangled, I caught up with friends
from childhood, saying *remember? remember?*

I remember it was a Thursday because I was buzzing
for Zumba and Ladies' Night at the Vic and I remember
reading about it on Facebook, thinking Australia
had already celebrated what was being called a coupe

and Julia Gillard, they said, had balls of steel, Julia
Gillard, they said, had an enormous ass—they said
arse, I say *ass*—and I popped a cola to celebrate her
flesh and her voice as our first female prime minister,
my calorie intake a minor nuisance, considering.

If I tell you I didn't know who to share the news with
it's because Australia was asleep and I didn't trust anyone
in America could be as happy and simultaneously nervous
as I, and the last thing I wanted was disappointment.
What I wanted was to hold it in before letting it out
and stop it from being about the media, but did those
good intentions make up for my cola? Nothing ever does.

I was seated by my computer at a small table in the corner
of a kitchen in the United States, reading about Prime
Minister Julia Gillard, and I'd do it every morning
after we returned from our travels, autumn settling in,
the eldest back at school, the baby down for her morning
nap, the middle child watching those octonaughts,
and it was *Julia's body* they kept measuring in perfect
black ink, *Julia's body* they needed to explain to the world.

I can't figure out what's wrong with me but the only thing
I dislike more than my body is disliking my body, and that's
about the media too, yet no matter how many calories
I swallow nearly half of my body will always be water,
just like everyone else's, and that should make us equal
though women are never equal. Julia couldn't *man-up*.
She knew it, I knew it and my mother knew it too.

If I tell you my mother worked in the court system
in 1970s America and wasn't even a secretary,
do I have to say that the men she tried to be equal to
talked about their penises and still got paid? I dream
of a day when women don't fear men and I can eat laksa

while wearing a white shirt and leave the restaurant
unstained. Neither of these seem possible, but at least
I can wear black while eating laksa—what can I do
about men at night when I'm using public transport?
No, really, *what can I do?* Because I'd like to pass it
onto my daughter, who's grown so big she takes the train
to the city without me, and to my sons, who are now men.

Children are our future, and the media weighed Julia
for never having them, either cold or unfuckable,
though I don't think that can be true of anyone.
Our bodies are made soft for holding. Heat happens
one way or another. Just imagine the hot flushes
she would've had between the ages of forty-eight
and fifty-one sitting as PM, but did she ever talk about
the desires of her raging vagina to those men,
and would the government have paid her if she did?

When my mother—who lives in America and I hope
doesn't die before a woman serves as US president—
asked me about Julia Gillard, I played it basic,
said she was determined to help sick people,
didn't mention the shape of her body.

My children and I are back in Australia, fourteen
years older. There are so many wars, so much fear,
knifings rampant, women battered—somewhere
a pregnant teenager is crying while a woman
looking down at the bloodstain on her knickers
is crying, and there's a newborn baby crying too.
I don't think our first female prime minister had balls
of steel because one, she did not have testicles
and two, can you imagine how exhausted you'd be
trying to please everyone and no one at the same time?

Tough gig, wish I could've taken your hand and led
you to the Vic, Jules. We'd let them call us ladies
if it was only for a night, especially if there was a dance
floor where we took turns in the middle of a circle
framed by a dozen cheering women. I'd lean over
and yell in your ear *I hope neither of us die before
a woman serves as the US president!* and you'd place
your hand on my shoulder and shout *I'll drink to that!*
We'd cheers without missing a beat, without spilling
a drop. In this dream, we can say and do whatever we want.

No Matter How Much Skin I Lose I Am Always the Same Body

I was shedding, stripped and blue-veined. It happens every few years,
and though I'm no soldier each time was an earnest battle. I was sick,
which led to the first backrub. I remember discussions of tin roofs,
no heat like Adelaide-heat and mimosas, flowers when a friend died.
I was reading a lot of grunge then, illness a new kind of sloughing,
an ecdysis. I bled. There were dogs, the park at midnight and when you
said you were falling in love with me I asked if I had to move out.
We kissed by the garden where cucumbers struggled under a dead
grapevine. There was acquiescence then, later wisteria, my skin
trailing behind us and you tripping over it. For a second I thought
we were in this together. You bathed me. There was ginger
in everything we ate. There was a couch that unfolded into a bed
which I lay on for aching hours while you went out into the world.
I wrote poems about sex and chilli peppers. When the winter rain
hit Adelaide we talked about tin roofs again. I'd grown new skin
that you liked to touch. It covered my body, which was mine.

the room closes in

1.
in front of the doorway's a mirror, it's critical positioning, there are sliver-thin streaks and a smudge by my head, I'm drowning in a pain of glass, I think it's me but I'm morphing, middle-aged a hyphenated word, I can't tell if the mirror is sniggering or snivelling beneath its silence, my skin has stories too, it's lived a really long time, the mirror doesn't recognise time though I've tried to introduce them, time + mirror = I come from somewhere deep inside, it's full of blood and forever moving, memory's like a crooner floating above me and around me, I'm always looking at myself, a monster's come to visit, it's getting crowded in here, ripple and swell, my child-self's confused, in the mirror her hand is touching my cheek, she doesn't understand the point of this, I could explain but my flesh has forced me mute, like history, like the black creases and craters that made the world.

2.
in front of the doorway's a mirror, I am always looking at myself, I could explain but my flesh has forced me mute, ripple and swell, I think it's me but I'm morphing, it's getting crowded in here, it's critical positioning, there are sliver-thin streaks and a smudge by my head, my skin has stories too, it's lived a really long time, time + mirror = history, the black creases and craters that made the world, I am always looking at myself, I can't tell if the mirror is sniggering or snivelling beneath its silence, a monster's come to visit, middle-aged is a hyphenated word, the mirror doesn't recognise time though I keep trying to introduce them, memory's like a crooner floating above me and around me, I am always looking at myself, I'm full of blood and forever moving, I come from somewhere deep inside, I'm drowning in a pain of glass, my child-self's confused, she doesn't understand the point of this, in the mirror her hand is touching my cheek.

3.

in front of the doorway's a mirror, ripple and swell, I can't tell if the mirror is sniggering or snivelling beneath its silence, middle-aged is a ten-letter word, I could explain but my flesh has forced me mute, like history, like the black creases and craters that made the world, it's getting crowded in here, there are sliver-thin streaks and a smudge by my head, my child-self's confused, in the mirror her hand is touching my cheek, she doesn't understand the point of this, of me drowning in a pane of glass, of me drowning in pain of glass, the mirror doesn't recognise time though I've tried to introduce them, memory's like a crooner floating above me and around me, it's critical positioning, a monster's come to visit, it's full of blood and forever moving, it's lived a really long time, I think it's me but I'm morphing, I come from somewhere deep inside, my skin has stories too, time + mirror = I am always looking at myself.

But It's Not Just When Your Period Stops

(These words—clipped, rearranged and formed anew—are the testimonies of ten women. Only tenses and pronouns have been changed.)

There is this profound physical and emotional thing that happens
to all women but it's completely ignored. I find that surprising and weird.
Girls don't really think about what it means; they should be educated.

The big silence, I was told nothing about it. During my sex education
it was completely glossed over, if not non-existent.
I've only recently learned menopause can go on for ten years.

> I am very tired, exhausted.
> My body doesn't feel
> like mine anymore.

It's like the car I'd been driving since new, kept in pristine condition
and having a great many miles left on the clock, suddenly fell apart.
The handle fell off the door, lights flashed erratically, the fuel consumption
shot through the roof and the brakes grated and shrieked. I was blowing
smoke but no-one seemed concerned: a breaking body losing control.

There's more of me in places there hasn't been before.
Breasts soften and drop and I've learnt what jowls are.
My relationship with my body is as tense as the body
itself is loose, deep annoyance at the thick and chunky.

> I'm uncomfortable.
> A physical disarray.

I am losing my body hair but growing a goatee
so you can imagine the astonishment at my discombobulation.
Strange curiosity, I need to find a new way to be with this emerging elder.
I do nothing to conceal my ageing. It's my new iteration.

There are TV shows, memes and jokes about it but I don't
find it very humorous. I've lost my confidence. I'm nervous
and the anxiety I didn't even know existed rises like fire or flood.

Then comes the insomnia, the broken sleep, broken dreams, broken energy.
I am profoundly muted and passionless, devastated to watch my sex life
diminish and waver. I've lost interest. No one ever told me.

My clitoris is a grain of rice, my vagina dry. Striving has lost
its grip for me, the on-switch disconnected. It's a pretty big shock
and I'm not sure the world is that interested.

Hot flushes, a racing heart, an anxious gallop.
My brain is a little more foggy than usual (bla bla bla) –
	the losses accumulate.

This is the biggest and most major overhaul in my entire life.
My gums bleed and teeth ache, my blood pressure skyrockets.

        It's bodily climate crisis.
        A long goodbye.
        I grieve.

I seem to be invisible—no, I'm *tolerated*. The lovely drug
of oestrogen drains from my body. Uptight and cranky,
I've lost the ability to string words together with ease;
the stories I've told myself about who I am no longer hold.

I think women are better than men, kinder, more thoughtful, more beautiful
and interesting and intelligent, but it still feels like the short straw.
I am working through the grief of loss and change every day.

It is true you stumble into it oblivious and unprepared, frantic, pole-axed.
Even doctors won't tell you it's 'the change' when so much is changing.
There is gaslighting, disengagement, assumptions and the pigeon-hole
of neurotic older woman. My voice feels shrill in the room.

Self-contempt and shame rise, but also anger. Trivialised as minor
and normal and natural, I could have used more science, fewer platitudes.

I read essays by post-menopausal women about giving up their jobs in their fifties,
just as they'd started to catch up after raising children and looked like they might be
within reach of their career goals. Retiring early because they 'couldn't cope'.

Depends on what you focus on, the rear-view mirror or what's in front of you.
Like I am invisible, but not invisible to other women going through this stage of life.
I feel like my body is telling me to see things differently, to understand
what else I might have to offer the world than just a socially acceptable form.

        That's a nice thought.

We get to take on another figure, a new look, and I love watching
older women stepping into their own. I've let my hair go grey as well
and I don't think people care too much. No one says anything.

        That's nice too.

Invisibility can afford you a strange unanticipated freedom.
I don't miss the sexual gaze. I like the clear cool space
of my un-sex-cluttered mind. I see things in a new, sober way.
I do not miss the relentless distraction of a libidinous impulse.
I do not miss my period.   But

my period has been a friend of sorts and she will be missed.
It's not about no longer being able to make babies, it's more
about an emotional passport my period has often afforded me.
Permission to withdraw and rest, to muse on the miracle of my body.

        An evolving flowering, oceanic renewal.
        A privilege reminding me of my womanness.

Have compassion, expect change, self-educate and advocate.
Talk about it. Demand that people talk about it. Step up the self-love.

Dance, celebrate and honour yourself more. Have courage. Grow large.

There is a secret comradery of older women who are wise
and will laugh with you and pour the wine, cheer with you, rage
with you, live imperfectly alongside you.

                You, a changeling.
        You, a crone.

'The Song Remains the Same'

Slammed against a reckless wall of cigarette smoke and pheromones, we were hot and hectic, all-in, full-on, randy and bucking, those squally times, our back-throat burns, cool car rides with Zepplin flaming—*If you can sing a guitar riff it's a classic fer sure*—and us so urgent and instantaneous, our fresh blood pumping to the brash night sky or all a-thrum in a weed-haze room, holding music inside our ribcages like speakers going thud and boom, us aglide, us athrust, not going home nor growing old, yet here we are, hair pluckers, sensitive teeth, sitting on the couch and reclining our feet, recalling the time when Robert Plant came to the Thebby, arched back like a mic-stand-fucker with seventy years in his skin and I said *That man is still a shit-hot rock god* and went on and on about how we age and remain the same and you said *Just like the song!*

Freezeframe the Bear

hush, quick, moment, history, the old leaves, the living hair, the worn path, my offspring, our heartbeats, (my heartbreak), round cub, eye-lock, shock-calm, big hand covers what's small, paw & claw, stuck & see, pine & dirt, scent of scat, confrontation, cease, be, the birdsong, the onlookers, tweet & crunch, my hot breath, nostril-twitch, core of the earth, pit of the cave, bounty of bark & sap & sun, the outdoors / no doors, the future this instant, *pass through, don't pass out*, tiptoe, boot, shuffle of the small, sleep of the baby on my back & there, beast, here, mama, here, chest, belly, eyes, open, eyes, open

'Pain cannot be told. Yet, in isolation, it grows.'

pain grows

(yet told, it grows   pain, yet told   pain in the morning
pain in the seepage on the stiff-cold sheets   pain in the told
in isolation pain grows)   (yet...)   (isolation in pain   &
the stiff-cold sheets   isolation in pain   &)   (&)

(isolation, it grows   it grows, yet told)   (clear your throat
– remember water—   isolation cannot be told)

(pain in the secret   delicate folds
      pain, it grows   pain (un)told)

(pain told isolation to grow, yet isolation cannot be told:
      cannot pain   cannot isolation)
                                      (cannot yet)   (yet
                                                             pain)

Softly

I've learned to speak softly to doctors so they trust my suffering
in the same way I trusted that the dead blackbird
outside the fourth doctor's window would not be opening its eyes.
Death is always there, but so is life. If a doctor stands
atop another one's shoulders and that doctor stands atop
another one's shoulders and so it goes until there's a doctor-chain
from Earth to Sun, could they breathe air back into the sky
as they would into lungs? Perhaps they could save us from ruin,
the northern quolls and our vineyards, too—
it's possible I fantasise doctors.

>(I also wonder if ghosts hide behind doctors' doors
>awaiting our arrivals because I could've sworn I
>felt a tickle on my external acoustic meatus as one
>slipped inside my ear.)

*

It's not like I want to be cured I said. *I'm for an illness that wakes up with me every morning, sometimes with arms like lengthy slugs across my chest, other times with hungover kisses. My illness is antediluvian; it's in my bones so I don't believe in severing it. I'm for a particular type of management.*

>*It's possible you're dehydrated* the doctor said.

That's not why I came (though I'd drunk a bottle of Shiraz the night before as I watched two movies back-to-back: a psychologist would have asked what the movies were while a sick person who'd drunk a bottle of Shiraz would've forgotten the names.)

*

This was the fourth doctor
to tell me the same as the first
and because I refuse to feel hopeless
I imagined him to be like me,
just a regular person who enjoys
occasional road trips and outings to pubs,
the type who has 'tequila stories'
because when you think tequila
is a promising idea you're most likely
already drunk

meaning: we all make mistakes.

It didn't work. He was so different from me
that my hopelessness was overwhelming.

> (Note: if your ever in a pub with this fourth doctor
> examine his confidence and order a shot of it.
> Slam it, pucker, squint from its heat and shiver.
> Ask yourself why you still don't feel better.)

*

It wasn't funny when he laughed at me.
Maybe it was his way of summarising the time
we had spent together. Some doctors are like creeks
with their clean rushing water: beautiful in their hurrying
towards an unseeable end.

*

I shouldn't have had to ask for the jellybean
as the printer spat out the paper I was to deliver
to the person scheduling my next appointment,
because they're meant for children.

I have doctor-friends who don't buy into the jellybean thing
though they admit to worshiping mystery and the body
(don't we all) and it's something I love about those friends
but it didn't raise my opinion of the fourth doctor
or lift my mood in any way—I lost my patience.

                      (If you're a criminal, admitting you don't know
                      means you most likely do; if you're a philosopher
                      or Buddhist, you are reaching your potential; if you're
                      a drunk, it means you've probably blacked-out
                      in the middle of the second movie and can't
                      remember the plot. If you're a doctor—
                      you can see how I lost my patience.)

*

Well I said, nearly in tears, *let's cross our fingers and drink to gloom* though there was no tequila in the room so I ate the jellybean I'd had to beg for, and then I smiled, softly.

When Things Fall Apart

When Things Fall Apart

1. You enter conversations with your lover halfway through, say *sorry, can you start again?*
2. Your face is hangdog with new angles.
3. You can't stop looking in the mirror though you know what happens when you look in mirrors.
4. You are sick of the build-up; you have been afraid before.
5. You notice yourself checking-in with yourself—*did that just happen, did it really just happen?*—quite certain that it did.
6. You tell your children to stop as soon as they start having fun, impatience like a bubbling stew muted from crust at the bottom of the pot.
7. You self-medicate.
8. You begin saying no to friends. Suddenly, all the time, you are saying no.
9. You slow down with the cleaning, the driving, the talking, the walking.
10. Your thoughts become one long rhyme.

When Things Fall Apart

1. You medicate.
2. You recognise your body, and when you rest your head on its chest and begin to sway, you remember its blood-rhythm.
3. You call your mother because it's prudent to cry.
4. You indulge in hot baths and pasta someone else has cooked.
5. Sex is slower, more desperate but softer, with deeper orgasms.
6. Strong in your fragility, you gratefully receive.
7. You think about identity because it's in question.
8. Feeling frail, you say *I am going to lie down* and do.
9. You read more, test your empathy radar, blitz it in repose.
10. You stroke your dog longer; it is clear the two of you have grown closer.

How to Heal Yourself

Barometric pressure drops fast
like a bullet felling for the third time
in two weeks its victim.

> *If it's your ears bothering you,*
> *surround yourself with silence.*
> *Failing that, mix apple cider vinegar*
> *with equal parts warm water*
> *and drop five tears into your ear—*
> *it'll sizzle and pop then calm.*
> *Try to avoid fervent winds;*
> *they don't give a stuff about you.*
> *Check for wax and bugs,*
> *which happen to love you.*

It's fire season fire
season fire fire season…

> *If your lips are cracked and dry*
> *balm them thickly while humming*
> *something catchy. If that doesn't help*
> *kiss your lover in their private parts.*

The smoke from the fire carries ash
landing greyer-than-my-dying-
aunt's-skin in my fragrant glass.
Homebrewed cider is a summertime
favourite with new woody overtones.

> *I'm no expert*
> *but I'd say if a nose is running*
> *don't run after it. Blow hard*
> *from the back of your throat*
> *and get yourself in front of it.*
> *Or bathe in eucalyptus,*

> *steam up the walls, wilt the corners*
> *of your poetry book—everything*
> *dries out eventually. Alternatively,*
> *try walking at dusk, good*
> *for the lungs by way of the nose.*

'I always forget my sunglasses' she laughed
as they rode off into the day.

> *If it's tired eyes, sleep.*
> *Or hold cold fingers to closed lids—*
> *it's as good as the first breath*
> *after chugging a half litre of water.*
> *It's as good as the water.*

Meanwhile, flooding up north,
streets of river, houses
drowning, think of mothers
clutching newborns,
all those animals.

> *Water & lemon for a sore throat,*
> *water & honey, water with roots*
> *of ginger, liquorice & marshmallow,*
> *a gargle of salt water, a bowl*
> *of week broth: healing is mostly*
> *about water, which is also lap*
> *of lip, the cry you hold in.*

Too much carbon dioxide in the air
means we'll melt into a history of obscurity:
'What was the name of that plant?'
No one around to ask.

> *If your chest is tight, generously*
> *sprinkle parsley on your food*
> *to break up mucus in the lungs.*
> *If desperate, pull your heart out*

> *and let it rest in the bedside drawer.*
> *Drink cough syrup until you hallucinate*
> *and begin to hear plants talking.*
> *Fall in love with the plants, it can't hurt.*
> *Speak to them in rhyme.*

Six channels dedicated to news
and on top of that, our screen feeds.
O the lives we never knew we'd lead!

> *A headache dulls the world,*
> *so watch for triggers:*
> *strong odours, caffeine, excessive stress—*
> *it's probably best to stop thinking.*

Crisis / Disease

Christ it's cracking-hot today
Here comes the cavorting wind
The spark crowds the crow's grass
The barometric cloud crash
Chaos cruising on a northerly
And clapping crying fire-babies
Castrated trees taking it up the trunk
The cul-de-sac being consumed
Cue the chopper and its drop
Contain it cover it clog it up
Charred now, clumps of coal

I think I'll sing a dizzy ditty
O, my dilapidated eardrum
Not-draining is so draining
I'm developing the dis
The dis-use of the useful
I'm a disoriented diva
This devastation of vessel
I develop dire dystopias
Drenched in the disproportionate
Get delirious with deification
Depression equals not done yet

Diagnosis and Treatment

There are singing shells in my ear; it is important to drink water.

Fluid-changes in the tubes cause aural fullness, a hurrying
of swollen rivers, corrugation in vomit-bowls.

Avoid salt and caffeine, chocolate, alcohol, ears shattered
in the wind; sit happily picking over, picking over.

In this condition: ringing plugged into quiet air,
vertigo held out to catch rains of sound, chronic creep
of nausea in high tide, episodes to take away.

Vestibular rehabilitation may ease the sensation of spinning on the shore
or your doctor may prescribe a diuretic broken beneath rain.

Your doctor may inject medication where the waters rise, causing loss
of balance by a cold deep sea, headaches of alluvial memory.

Bath Towel

One day you will walk outside, become lost in familiarity,
finally understand the clouds aren't trying to melt you.

You will turn the corner, pass someone and feel the thump,
know your heartbeat belongs to you but also to the throng.

In this city you will pass health clinics, petrol stations,
people who look you in the eye: we call this freedom.

Keep walking. Cars will avoid you if you avoid them,
most animals too, especially those nocturnal ones.

Come night you'll be tired, your body will ache and seek
nourishment and remember. It's what guts and bones do.

Your body will try to catch what's running
and it'll drive you mad. Maybe you'll fall in love

and love will drive you mad. Maybe love will splatter
on the road from a car that failed to avoid it.

Maybe you'll buy your own car; maybe you'll buy love.
One day you will enter a place that wasn't built for you

but you'll give it your name, dishes, a couch, a shower caddy.
Each shower will wash you clean but you'll continue to get dirty.

Skin is a craving thing, touch filthy. Because the bath towel
will dry your body, keep it fresh and soft. I know people

who've had their initials embroidered onto bath towels.
This world is full of poems, so you can do that too.

Some Questions I Ask Myself When I Cannot Sleep

A question I ask myself when I cannot sleep is
What does a middle-aged body look like?
I am a vision of my past's future
but I never imagined to grow so strange.
Heave and roll and overflow, I have to re-learn sitting
because the middle-aged woman gains fat,
loses muscle, stores the world in her abdomen
where she might have stored it before
if she'd ever been pregnant. Back then
her body would've been celebrated.
People would've looked at it and smiled.

What does a middle-aged body sound like? I ask.
My partner tells me I snore. My estrogen is fading
and the soft tissue in my throat has slackened
so I cannot sleep on my back or with a hand resting
on my neck unless I don't mind being rude, and for months,
after I had COVID and coughed constantly with great force,
I thought my vagina might fall from my body and slop
to the kitchen floor, its living waste seeping into the cracks
of our wooden slats with the dirt blown-in from the outside, the dander
of our long-dead dog, remnants of mice poo and the antennas of flies
we swatted and killed—all the organic stuff. My estrogen is fading
and the soft tissue of everything you think of when you hear the words
down there has loosened. Goddess, grant me a strong pair of knickers
and make them black to hide my gaffes.

I've gone off track but I tend to do that. I should've asked
What does a middle-aged woman worry about?
before I dove into prolapse. Or at least answered the question like this:
the middle-aged body sounds like footsteps rushing to the toilet.

I interrogate desire, which is a hand cupped around,
though not touching, genitals.
Must I keep talking about genitals?
During menopause, when estrogen drops and wanes,
there is less blood supply to the vagina
and I have to talk about vaginas when I say
it can be harder to become aroused. There's dryness.
Again and again, the tissue of the vagina will thin.
It's called atrophy. Go on, say it: *va-gi-nal a-tro-phy*.
Not everyone's the same. Some desire their lovers more,
which is mirrored in the steam of opposing breaths crashing
onto a windowpane. Desire's a full well with a heavy bucket
sploshing its water all over your body before you swallow.
I think of it in liquid form, as I would a vagina
but sometimes can't, thanks to lowered estrogen levels.

When I ask myself if desire sounds like anything particular
I answer: *Only the obvious, what you'd expect, birth and death
thrashing in one's gullet then escaping in unforeseen song.*

When insomnia hits, I ask myself if I'd like to escape.
Some days I don't know what else to do but read.
I eat books and salivate over the ones I've yet to devour.
The last time I felt this intensely about literature I was a teenager,
estrogen pouring into my body like rain from a tank's unfiltered tap,
its goodness moulding my breasts, widening my hips,
covering my humid places with hair and making me a secret.
Also this: the last time I had these migraines I was a teenager,
new estrogen unbalancing me like lightning tipping the sky.
You see, women are multi-taskers because we've always adapted
to changes in estrogen during the many stages of our lives,
during the various stages of each month, during every minute
of every day. Our body is always doing something with hormones
while it does something else with a ladle or spade,
a phone or a car, a computer, a baby, a book.
Rather than escape, I'd like to simply simplify.

But what does simple mean? I ask.
There is no answer, everything's complex
but some days I don't leave my house.
I wear only my bathrobe, nothing else.
My bathrobe is blue. I roll up the sleeves
while swirling five drops of oil
into the water of my bath. Only when I'm done
do I discard my robe. It lands in a soft pile at my feet.
I step into the tub and when I sit down
the water rushes over my pelvis like a river
over a sunken boulder, wild and clean.
Then the movement settles, which means my body
has been accepted. I lie back, slide underwater,
come up to breathe, and it's just so good to breathe.

Notes

p.60: 'Pain cannot be told. Yet, in isolation, it grows' title taken from the essay 'The Listening Room' by Lara Birk in the anthology *Stories of Illness and Healing: Women Write Their Bodies*, which can be viewed at https://www.thesagepractice.com/

p.69: This is a found poem sourced from https://www.healthline.com/health/menieres-disease#symptoms and Laura Riding Jackson's poem 'Ears'

Acknowledgements

These poems were predominantly written on the lands of the Kaurna people and the Ngarrindjeri people of South Australia. Sovereignty was never ceded.

'A Conversation about Art'—*Rabbit*: Art issue.

'After Suzanne Duchamp's *Young Woman with Dog*'—*Australian Poetry Anthology, 2024*.

'Bobo'—*Voluminous Grid: An Adelaide Poetry App* (eds. Aidan Coleman and Thom Sullivan).

'Briefly'—University of Canberra Health Prize shortlist and anthology.

'But how did the hole get there?'—*Antipodes* (US).

'But It's Not Just When Your Period Stops'—Red Room Poetry commission

'Crisis / Disease'—*Sunder*.

'Dancing to Flo Rida with Julia Gillard'—*Australian Poetry Anthology, 2025*.

'Diagnosis and Treatment'—*Bramble*.

'Games'—*Overland*.

'Hello / Goodbye'—*Locative*.

'Holding Water', 'We Have to try harder to stop trying so hard' and 'When You Go We Are Left'—*RiveraineMuse* (India).

'House on Stilts'—*Stylus Lit*.

'No Matter How Much Skin I Lose I Am Always the Same Body'—*Not Very Quiet* and *Best Australian Poetry* 2021.

'Nothing out of the Ordinary'—*Overland*.

'Softly'—*Australian Poetry Journal: Divergence/relevance*.

'Spoonbridge and Cherry at the Opening of a Toilet'—*Cordite: Pop issue*.

'the room closes in'—*Saltbush Review*.

About the Author

Heather Taylor-Johnson's works spanning novels, autofiction, poetry, memoir and essays have been recognised in the Readings Prize for Fiction, *ABR*'s Calibre Prize, *Island*'s Nonfiction Prize and the Newcastle Poetry Prize. A South Australian Arts Fellow and recipient of residencies at Bundanon, Varuna and the Whitlam Institute, and overseas residencies at the Anderson Centre in Minnesota and the Keesing Studio in Paris, Heather's writing explores themes of belonging, illness, and art. She's the editor of *Shaping the Fractured Self: Poetry of Chronic Illness and Pain* and is an adjunct research fellow at the JM Coetzee Centre for Creative Practice.

About the artist

Born in Poland and reborn in Australia, D-Mo moves between worlds—an international visual storyteller proving that identity is built, not given. She tells stories through the body, through memory, and through the quiet battles most people never see. Her portraits reveal a truth we all feel but rarely name: the human spirit does not freeze in place. It adapts. It rises. It grows stronger. That is why her work resonates around the world.

The real question is simple: who are you becoming when life demands you change?

Cover image: 'I Lost Someone Then Found Them In My Body'

If the body remembers everything—what part of you is trying to rise now that loss has cleared the space?

www.ingramcontent.com/pod-product-compliance
Lightning Source LLC
Chambersburg PA
CBHW020546080526
44583CB00013B/1021